Jefferson Fisher New Book 2025

Tools to Speak Up, Stay Grounded, and Lead with Emotional Intelligence in a Noisy World

Copyright © 2025

All rights reserved. No part of this publication may be reproduced, distributed, or transmitted in any form or by any means, including photocopying, recording, or other electronic or mechanical methods, without the prior written permission of the publisher, except in the case of brief quotations embodied in critical reviews and certain other noncommercial uses permitted by copyright law.

Table of Contents

Table of Contents 3
   Chapter One 10
   Why We Argue in the First Place 10
      The Real Reason We Argue 11
      The Hidden Conflict Cycle 13
      Why This Matters 14
   Chapter Two 16
   Regulate Before You Relate 16
      The Power of Regulation 17
      Why It's So Hard When You're Triggered .. 18
      Tools to Regulate in Real Time 19
         1. Name It to Tame It 19
         2. Breathe Like You Mean It 20
         3. Feel Your Feet 21
         4. Take a Pause, Not a Punishment 21
         5. Check the Story You're Telling Yourself 22
      From Reacting to Responding 23
      Final Thoughts 24
   Chapter Three 25
   The Pause That Changes Everything 25
      Why the Pause Feels So Unnatural 26
      What the Pause Actually Does 27
         1. It Breaks the Emotional Spiral 27
         2. It Signals Confidence and Self-Containment 28

3. It Invites the Other Person to Reflect.. 28

4. It Clarifies What Matters Most......... 28

Practicing the Pause: What It Looks Like.. 29

⬢ The Emotional Pause.................... 29

◼ The Reflective Pause.....................30

⬢ The Power Pause.......................... 30

Silence Doesn't Mean Disengagement..... 31

The Hidden Wisdom of Silence................. 32

Final Thoughts.. 33

Chapter Four... 34

The Voice in Your Head.................................. 34

The Fight Doesn't Start With Them—It Starts Inside You... 35

What Is a "Fight Script"?........................... 36

Step 1: Identify Your Script....................... 37

Step 2: Pause and Question the Narrative 38

Step 3: Rewrite the Script Before You Speak 39

Your Voice Shapes the Conversation........ 41

The Healing Power of a Rewritten Script.. 42

Final Thoughts.. 43

Chapter Five..44

Stop Reacting, Start Responding................... 44

Reaction Is Survival. Response Is Leadership.. 45

The Pause Makes All the Difference......... 46

Intentional Language Builds Safer Conversations... 48

Know Your Triggers So You Can Catch the Spiral... 49

Replace Impulse with Curiosity................50
Teach Your Body a New Way to Speak.....52
Responding Isn't Weak. It's Brave............53
Final Thoughts...53
Chapter Six...55
Speak with Clarity, Not Confusion...................55
Why We Water Down What We Want........56
The Power of Clear, Concise Communication..57
Examples of Clarity vs. Confusion............58
How to Craft Clear, Boundary-Based Phrases..59
Why Short Phrases Work..........................60
Practice: Own Your Words with "I" Statements...61
When Clarity Meets Compassion..............62
Final Thought: Clarity Creates Connection...62

Chapter Seven...64
Boundaries Without Walls...............................64
Why Boundaries Matter.............................65
The Challenge: Saying No Without Guilt...65
Saying No With Strength and Compassion...66
    1. Be Clear and Direct..........................66
    2. Use "I" Statements...........................67
    3. Express Appreciation.......................67
    4. Offer Alternatives When Possible....67
Turning Discomfort Into Confidence..........68
Real Talk: Boundaries Don't Always Please Everyone..68

- Practice: Simple Boundary Phrases to Start With 69
- When Boundaries Build Connection 70
- Final Thought: Your Boundaries Are an Act of Love 71

Chapter Eight 72
Listen to Understand, Not to Win 72
- Why We Don't Really Listen 73
- What Does Listening to Understand Look Like? 73
- Replacing Rebuttals With Reflection 74
- Becoming the Calmest Person in the Room. 75
- Why This Changes Everything 76
- Practice: Active Listening Prompts 77
- Real Talk: Listening Doesn't Mean Agreeing 78
- Final Thought: Listening Is Love in Action 78

Chapter Nine 79
Control Is an Illusion 79
- Why Trying to "Fix" or "Convince" Doesn't Work 80
- What Real Influence Looks Like 81
- The Freedom of Letting Go 82
- Practical Tips for Letting Go of Control in Conversation 82
- Real Talk: Influence Is a Process, Not a Power Move 83
- Final Thought: Control Is Overrated, Connection Isn't 84

Chapter Ten 85

Emotional Weight vs. Emotional Honesty........ 85
   Emotional Honesty: The Gift of Clarity and Trust.......... 86
   Emotional Weight: When Sharing Becomes Overload............87
   How to Share Honestly Without Overexposing............ 88
   Why This Matters.......... 89
   Real Talk: Vulnerability Isn't About Overloading..........89
   Practice: Emotional Honesty Framework.. 90
   Final Thought: Honesty with Heart Creates Connection............ 90

Chapter Eleven.......... 92
Navigating Difficult People Calmly.......... 92
   Calm Is Your Superpower.......... 93
   Types of Difficult People and Their Tactics... 93
   Tools to Keep Your Cool............94
   Protecting Your Energy.......... 96
   Reminder: Calm Isn't Compliance............97
   Practice: Go-to Phrases for Calm Power.. 97
   Final Thought: Don't Let Chaos Inside You... 99

Chapter Twelve............ 100
Hard Conversations Without the Drama....... 100
   Why Hard Conversations Spiral.......... 101
   Step-by-Step: The Calm Conversation Method............ 102
      Step 1: Get Clear on Why You're Speaking Up..........102

Step 2: Choose the Right Moment.... 102
  Step 3: Open Gently, Not Defensively..... 103
  Step 4: Use "I" Language, Not "You" Accusations... 103
  Step 5: Be Specific and Simple......... 104
  Step 6: Pause for Their Response.... 104
  Step 7: Stay Grounded If It Gets Heated. 105
  Step 8: End With Mutual Respect..... 105
 What to Say When You're Scared to Bring It Up..106
 Final Thought: Keep the Door Open, Not the Drama... 107
Chapter Thirteen... 108
Repairing After Rupture................................ 108
 Why Rupture Happens........................... 109
 The Myth of the "Perfect Apology"...........110
 Step-by-Step: The Respectful Repair Method.. 110
  Step 1: Own It Fully........................... 110
  Step 2: Validate Their Experience......111
  Step 3: Apologize Without Self-Erasure.. 111
  Step 4: Don't Over-Explain or Justify. 112
  Step 5: Ask, Don't Assume................ 112
  Step 6: Change the Behavior............ 113
 What If They're Still Upset?..................... 114
 Self-Respect in the Repair Process........ 114
 Final Thought: Rupture Isn't the End....... 116
Chapter Fourteen.. 117

- Leading with Calm in Any Room.................... 117
  - Why Calm Is Magnetic............................. 118
  - What Leading with Calm Looks Like........ 119
  - Practice 1: Ground Before You Enter...... 119
  - Practice 2: Anchor to Your Values, Not Their Volume.. 120
  - Practice 3: Speak Low, Speak Slow........ 121
  - Practice 4: Make Space for Silence........ 122
  - Practice 5: Own Your Energy.................. 122
  - Calm Is Not Passive—It's Intentional...... 123
  - Leading with Calm Changes the Room... 124
- Chapter Fifteen... 125
- Your Voice, Fully Activated............................. 125
  - What It Means to Be "Fully Activated"..... 126
  - The Three Elements of Voice Activation. 127
  - Speaking Up: No More Shrinking............ 127
  - Setting Limits: Boundaries That Sound Like You... 129
  - Showing Up: Using Your Voice When It Counts... 130
  - Activating Your Voice in Everyday Moments. 131
  - Your Voice Is a Gift—Use It..................... 131
  - Final Thought... 132

Chapter One

Why We Argue in the First Place

The unseen root of most conflict
Why logic rarely wins emotional battles

Most arguments don't start with a screaming match.
 They begin quietly—with a moment of misunderstanding, a tone that rubs the wrong way, a look that feels like judgment, or a question that sounds like an accusation.

And just like that, the room gets ten degrees colder.

You know this moment. You've lived it. Maybe it was your partner rolling their eyes while you tried to explain yourself. Or a friend who interrupted you one too many times. Or a coworker who "wasn't trying to be rude" but very much was.

You take a breath. Try to stay calm.

But your chest tightens. Your heart speeds up. And before you know it, you're in it—defending, correcting, justifying, or retreating. You're arguing, not just with words, but with your **nervous system.**

The Real Reason We Argue

We don't argue because we disagree.

We argue because we feel **unseen**, **unheard**, or **disrespected**—and we want to **protect ourselves.**

Most conflict isn't about what's being said. It's about **what's being felt.**

It's not really about whose turn it was to do the dishes. It's about feeling like the other person doesn't value your time.

It's not about the calendar mix-up. It's about feeling left out, like you're not a priority.

When you peel back the surface, the root of most arguments is the same:

A need that hasn't been met.

An emotion that hasn't been named.

A hurt that hasn't been healed.

And yet, in the middle of these moments, what do we tend to do?

We reach for **logic**.

We list facts. We make our case. We quote what the other person said. We get louder, clearer, more determined—thinking if we could just explain it *right*, they'd understand and stop acting the way they are.

But here's the truth:

> **Logic rarely works when emotion is in charge.**

You can't out-argue someone's hurt feelings with bullet points.

You can't calm someone down by proving why they shouldn't be upset.

Think of it this way: If someone is drowning in a pool of emotion, giving them a lecture on how to swim better isn't going to help. They need a hand, not a theory.

We argue because we think we're fighting over a point.
But really, we're fighting over a feeling.

The Hidden Conflict Cycle

Let's break it down:

1. **Something triggers us.**

    A tone, a word, a gesture—it hits a nerve we didn't even know was raw.

2. **We feel threatened or misunderstood.**

    Our bodies enter protection mode: fight, flight, freeze, or fawn.

3. **We respond with logic or defensiveness.**

    We try to control the moment by being "right."

4. **They do the same.**

    And now it's not about what happened—it's about **who wins.**

Sound familiar?

The good news is: Once you see this pattern, you can change it.

You can pause, ground yourself, and **respond with clarity instead of reactivity.**

But that comes later.

First, we need to really understand something:

> **Arguing isn't always a sign of disrespect.**
>
> Sometimes it's just a sign of two people trying to protect their emotional safety in messy, imperfect ways.

Why This Matters

If we don't understand *why* we argue, we'll keep trying to solve the wrong problem.

We'll keep throwing logic at emotions.
We'll keep escalating instead of de-escalating.
We'll keep wondering why the other person "just doesn't get it," while they wonder the same about us.

This chapter isn't here to judge you. It's here to hold a mirror up and say:

You're not broken. You're just wired for protection.
And so is everyone else.

But there's a better way.
And it starts with learning how to speak in a way that **calms**, **connects**, and **clarifies.**

That's where we're headed next.

Chapter Two

Regulate Before You Relate

Why emotional control is your real superpower
Techniques to stay calm when triggered

Think of the last time you were in an argument and said something you later regretted.

Maybe your voice got louder than you intended.
Maybe you rolled your eyes, stormed off, or shut down.
Maybe you thought, *Why did I do that? I didn't even mean half of what I said.*

Here's the truth:
You probably weren't really "you" in that moment.
You were your nervous system in survival mode.

And when your nervous system takes the wheel, connection flies out the window.

The Power of Regulation

Before we can connect, we have to calm.
Before we can speak clearly, we have to feel safe.
Before we can relate, we have to regulate.

Emotional regulation is the ability to manage what's happening inside you before it spills out onto the people around you. It's what turns a tense conversation into a healing one.
It's what helps you pause instead of pounce.
It's what allows you to be the grown-up in the room—even when your inner child is having a meltdown.

This isn't about bottling up your feelings or pretending everything is fine.
It's about staying rooted when the storm hits.
It's about being able to say, *"I'm upset, but I'm still in control."*

**Emotional regulation is not suppression.
It's self-leadership.**

And it's a muscle—one that gets stronger every time you choose to stay with your feelings without being ruled by them.

Why It's So Hard When You're Triggered

Let's be honest—staying calm sounds great... until someone hits a nerve.

When you're triggered, your brain sends out an internal emergency alert:

"Danger! You're not safe! Protect yourself!"

You feel heat in your chest, tension in your jaw, your breath shortens.

Your body is preparing to fight, flee, freeze, or fawn—even if the "danger" is just a sharp comment from your partner or a passive-aggressive text from a coworker.

And in that moment, your **thinking brain goes offline.**

You're not interested in connection.

You want to win. Escape. Defend. Or shut down.

This is normal. It's biology.

But it doesn't have to run your life.

You don't have to let a 90-second emotional wave ruin your day—or your relationship.

Tools to Regulate in Real Time

So how do you regulate? How do you stay grounded when your body wants to explode, retreat, or collapse?

Here are tools that work—not just in theory, but in the mess of real-life moments:

1. Name It to Tame It

When emotion rises, say to yourself:

"I'm feeling angry."

"I'm feeling scared."

"I'm feeling rejected."

Labeling the emotion gives your brain language—and calms your nervous system. It shifts you from reaction to reflection.

> The moment you name the feeling, you start to regain power over it.

2. Breathe Like You Mean It

You've heard it before: *"Just breathe."*

But here's how to make it work:

- Inhale for 4 counts

- Hold for 2

- Exhale slowly for 6 to 8 counts

Do this three times.

Why it works: Slow exhalation tells your body you're safe. It activates the parasympathetic nervous system—your body's calm button.

3. Feel Your Feet

Yes, really.

Ground yourself physically by bringing awareness to the soles of your feet. Wiggle your toes. Press down into the floor.

It might sound simple, but it reconnects your body to the present—and away from the mental spiral.

4. Take a Pause, Not a Punishment

If you feel flooded with emotion, **you can step away without storming out.**

Say something like:

"I want to talk about this, but I need a moment to calm down."

"Let me come back to this in five minutes when I can think more clearly."

This isn't avoidance—it's maturity.

You're not running. You're regulating.

5. Check the Story You're Telling Yourself

Most triggers come with a storyline:

"They don't respect me."

"I always have to be the one who cares more."

"They're trying to control me."

Ask yourself:

- Is this story true?

- Is it helpful?

- What else might be going on?

This mental pause lets you challenge assumptions before they ignite unnecessary conflict.

From Reacting to Responding

The gap between **reaction** and **response** is where your power lives.

Regulation gives you that gap.

It lets you **choose** how you want to show up instead of letting your emotional autopilot take over.

This is where real connection begins—not with being right, but with being calm enough to **see the other person** clearly.

Because when you can stay grounded, you become safe for others—even when the conversation is hard.

And that kind of presence?
It's magnetic. Disarming. Transformative.

Final Thoughts

You don't have to be perfect at this.
You just have to start noticing.

When you catch yourself getting pulled into an emotional riptide, remember:
You can pause.
You can breathe.
You can lead your emotions, instead of letting them lead you.

That's what regulation is.
And it's what makes connection possible—even in the middle of conflict.

Chapter Three

The Pause That Changes Everything

How silence creates space and authority
Using the pause to regain control in tough conversations

Let's begin with a counterintuitive truth:

The most powerful person in the room isn't the one who speaks first. It's the one who pauses.

Think about the last time you felt cornered in a conversation—when someone said something sharp, unfair, or flat-out wrong. Your body probably wanted to react instantly.

To defend. To correct. To explain.

To fill the silence before it became uncomfortable.

But here's the secret:

Silence is not weakness.

It's not avoidance.

And it's certainly not surrender.

The pause is presence.

It's where self-respect lives.

It's where emotional control shows up.

It's the moment you reclaim your ability to choose—not react.

Why the Pause Feels So Unnatural

Pausing in a heated moment is hard.
We're wired for speed, not stillness.

Most of us learned early on that silence = danger. That if we didn't respond quickly, we'd lose the argument, the respect, the job, or the relationship.

So we filled space with words—any words—just to feel in control.

But here's the irony:

In rushing to speak, we often lose the very control we're trying to gain.

We speak too soon.

We say what we don't mean.

We shut the other person down—or shut ourselves off.

When we pause, though?

We shift from *survival* to *strategy*.

What the Pause Actually Does

Let's look at what happens during a meaningful pause:

1. It Breaks the Emotional Spiral

A pause interrupts the rising tide of emotion. It buys your nervous system time to settle so your thinking brain can come back online.

2. It Signals Confidence and Self-Containment

When you can sit with silence, you're no longer performing. You're present. You're grounded. That confidence is felt—even if you say nothing at all.

3. It Invites the Other Person to Reflect

Pausing gives *them* space to reconsider, clarify, or soften. Silence often encourages self-correction better than any interruption ever could.

4. It Clarifies What Matters Most

In that small pocket of space, you can ask yourself:

- *What's really happening here?*

- *What do I actually want from this conversation?*

- *Is what I'm about to say going to help—or hurt?*

Practicing the Pause: What It Looks Like

This doesn't mean turning every conversation into a chess match. It means learning to **slow down** the moment before you speak or react.

Here are three ways to use the pause intentionally:

⬢ The Emotional Pause

> *When you feel yourself getting triggered*

Instead of reacting, try this inner script:

> *"I feel myself heating up. Let me pause before I speak."*

Take one full breath. Count to three in your head. Let the silence hold.

This doesn't just protect your words—it preserves your relationships.

■ **The Reflective Pause**

> *When someone says something confusing, vague, or emotionally loaded*

Let the words land.

Don't rush to fix, judge, or respond.

Try simply saying:

> *"Hmm."*
>
> *"Let me think about that for a second."*
>
> *"I want to make sure I understand what you mean."*

The pause gives you time to interpret, not just respond. That's where empathy and clarity begin.

● **The Power Pause**

> *When someone challenges you or expects a fast answer*

Rather than answering right away, try something like:

> *"That's an important question."*
>
> *"I want to give that the thought it deserves."*
>
> *"I'm going to take a moment before I respond."*

Watch how the dynamic shifts. You go from reactive to deliberate. From pressured to powerful.

Silence Doesn't Mean Disengagement

Let's be clear: pausing isn't stonewalling. It's not the cold shoulder.

It's not shutting down.

It's not withholding to punish.

It's tuning in—to yourself and the moment.

It says:

> *"I value this conversation enough not to rush it."*
>
> *"I value myself enough not to betray my clarity."*

In emotionally charged conversations, that kind of restraint is rare—and deeply impactful.

The Hidden Wisdom of Silence

Some of the most healing moments in communication come not from what is said, but from the space between the words.

- The moment you pause instead of snapping back.

- The second you take a breath instead of taking a jab.

- The space where something wiser than your anger has a chance to speak.

That's not silence. That's **leadership**.

And whether you're a partner, parent, boss, or friend, your ability to pause becomes a gift—to yourself and to everyone around you.

Final Thoughts

Learning to pause is like learning to see in the dark.
At first, it feels unnatural. Uncomfortable. Even risky.
But in time, you'll begin to notice something profound:

That silence can say, *"I'm calm."*
It can say, *"I'm listening."*
It can say, *"I'm not here to win—I'm here to connect."*

In a noisy world, a thoughtful pause speaks volumes.

Chapter Four

The Voice in Your Head

Identifying your internal "fight script"
Rewriting the story before you speak

Before the words leave your mouth—before the sigh, the eye roll, the comeback—something else has already spoken.

Your internal voice.

It's the quiet (or not-so-quiet) narrator that interprets everything before it hits your conscious mind.

It says things like:

- *"They don't respect me."*

- *"Here we go again..."*

- *"I always have to explain myself."*

- *"Why do I even bother?"*

And if we're not aware of this inner dialogue, it becomes the **invisible script** driving every fight, misunderstanding, and broken connection.

The Fight Doesn't Start With Them—It Starts Inside You

Have you ever entered a conversation already feeling tense—even though nothing's actually happened yet?

That's your inner script talking.
 It's already told you what to expect, what's going to go wrong, and why you need to stay on guard.

It's like walking into a room wearing armor before anyone has even raised a weapon.

And here's the truth:

If we want to change the way we communicate, we first have to change what we *believe* is happening.

Because your nervous system doesn't just respond to what's said—it responds to what *you think it means.*

What Is a "Fight Script"?

A fight script is the default story your brain runs during conflict or tension. It's shaped by past experiences, trauma, childhood dynamics, and repeated patterns.

Think of it like a reflex:

- Someone raises their voice → *"They're attacking me."*

- Someone goes quiet → *"They're punishing me."*

- Someone disagrees → *"They think I'm stupid."*

These scripts are protective—but also destructive.
They fill in the blanks with assumptions, not facts.
They cause us to react to old pain in new situations.

Step 1: Identify Your Script

The first step is **awareness**. You can't change what you don't notice.

Ask yourself:

- What's the story I tell myself when I feel hurt or disrespected?

- Do I jump to conclusions before I ask questions?

- What pattern do I see in most of my conflicts?

Common inner scripts include:

- *"I'm not being heard."*

- *"They always blame me."*

- *"I have to be right."*

- *"If I let this go, I'll look weak."*

- *"They're trying to control me."*

These beliefs may not be conscious—but they're loud. They sit just below the surface and leak into your tone, posture, and words.

Step 2: Pause and Question the Narrative

When you catch that script running, ask yourself:

"Is this 100% true—or just familiar?"

Because familiarity isn't fact. It's memory dressed as reality.

Try replacing judgment with curiosity.
Instead of:

"They don't care about me."
Try:
"What am I assuming right now?"
"What else might be going on for them?"

This doesn't mean excusing harmful behavior. It means **slowing down the story** so you can respond wisely instead of reacting wildly.

Step 3: Rewrite the Script Before You Speak

Imagine if you could edit your reaction *before* it ever became a conflict.

That's what emotional fluency is: rewriting the script before the words come out.

Instead of saying:

- *"You never listen to me."*
  Try:

- *"I'm feeling unheard right now. Can we slow down?"*

Instead of:

- *"You always twist my words."*
  Try:

- *"Can I clarify what I meant before we go further?"*

Instead of:

- *"You're doing this on purpose."*
  Try:

- *"I'm having a strong reaction, and I need a second to understand why."*

See the difference?

The first examples protect your ego.

The second examples protect the relationship.

Your Voice Shapes the Conversation

The story you tell yourself becomes the story you bring into every interaction.

So what if you chose a different story?

- One where you believe people aren't enemies, but confused or overwhelmed.

- One where you trust yourself enough to not need to dominate.

- One where your goal is not to "win," but to connect.

That shift changes everything—not just what you say, but *how you feel* saying it.

The Healing Power of a Rewritten Script

When you rewrite your internal dialogue, you stop being a prisoner of your past patterns.

You stop reacting to ghosts from old relationships.
You stop fighting battles that don't need to be fought.
You stop defending yourself from people who aren't trying to hurt you.

You speak softer.
You listen better.
You feel safer.

And that makes *everyone* around you safer too.

Final Thoughts

The voice in your head will always be there.
But it doesn't have to be the loudest voice in the room.

You can learn to hear it, question it, and rewrite it—moment by moment.

Because communication isn't just about what you say to others.
It's about what you're constantly saying to *yourself*—and whether that voice is healing or harming you.

Chapter Five

Stop Reacting, Start Responding

Shifting from defense to conscious choice
How to speak with intention, not impulse

When a conversation turns tense, we usually do one of two things:

We lash out. Or we shut down.

That's reacting.
And most of us are far better at it than we'd like to admit.

Reacting is fast.
It's emotional.

It's fueled by old habits, fears, and the automatic parts of our brain trying to keep us safe.

But reacting rarely makes us feel safe.

Instead, it escalates conflict, creates distance, and leaves us wondering, *"Why did I say that?"*

What we truly need—what transforms communication—is **responding.**

Responding is slower.
It's grounded.
It comes from the version of you that's calm, present, and wise.

Let's explore the shift.

Reaction Is Survival. Response Is Leadership.

When you react, you're not communicating from clarity. You're communicating from defense.

It might sound like:

- "You always do this!"

- "I'm done explaining myself."

- "Whatever. Believe what you want."

That's your nervous system trying to survive the moment, not connect through it.

But when you **respond**, something different happens.

You choose your words.
 You regulate your tone.
  You stay connected to your values—even when you're frustrated.

Reaction is instinct. Response is intention.

The Pause Makes All the Difference

You can't respond if you don't give yourself a *beat*—a moment of space between trigger and reply.

That's where clarity lives.

That pause might be one deep breath.
 Or it might be: "Can we take a break and come back to this in ten minutes?"

It doesn't have to be long. It just has to be **long enough to choose a better path**.

In that pause, ask yourself:

- What is this really about?

- What do I want from this conversation?

- Will what I'm about to say help or hurt?

That's how you shift from unconscious reaction to conscious communication.

Intentional Language Builds Safer Conversations

When you speak from reaction, your words often carry heat: blame, sarcasm, defensiveness.

But when you speak with **intention**, your tone softens—even if your message is firm.

Instead of saying:

- "You never listen to me,"
  Try:

- "I'm feeling unheard, and I'd like to feel more connected."

Instead of:

- "You're impossible,"
  Try:

- "I'm getting overwhelmed. Can we slow this down?"

Instead of:

- "I'm not dealing with this right now,"
  Try:

- "I need a minute to gather my thoughts so we can talk productively."

The goal isn't to sugarcoat.

The goal is to **stay in control of your emotional presence** while being honest.

Know Your Triggers So You Can Catch the Spiral

Every person has emotional buttons—words, tones, behaviors that set them off.

Take time to notice:

- What *types* of situations push you to react?

- Do you have patterns of defensiveness, shutting down, or over-explaining?

- What emotions tend to rise fastest—anger, shame, fear?

Knowing your triggers doesn't make them disappear. But it **gives you a heads-up** when you're entering reactive territory.

And once you notice it, you can choose:

> Do I let this hijack me—or do I pause and respond with purpose?

Replace Impulse with Curiosity

One of the fastest ways to move out of reaction is to ask a question—not just of the other person, but of yourself.

Instead of:

> "How dare they say that?"

Try:

> "What might be going on for them that I don't see?"

Instead of:

> "Why am I always the one to fix things?"

Try:

> "What boundary do I need here to protect my energy?"

Asking the *right questions* creates space.
Space brings calm.
And calm helps you respond like the version of you you're proud of.

Teach Your Body a New Way to Speak

Let's be real: your body speaks before your mouth does.

So part of learning to respond, not react, is retraining your **physical responses** in conflict.

Try:

- Loosening your shoulders

- Relaxing your jaw

- Uncrossing your arms

- Slowing your breathing

These signals tell your nervous system, *"I'm not in danger."* And when your body believes that, your brain doesn't have to go into survival mode.

Which means your words can come from strength, not fear.

Responding Isn't Weak. It's Brave.

A lot of people think "responding" means being passive or letting things slide.

Absolutely not.

Responding means:

- Speaking clearly and kindly

- Holding boundaries without blaming

- Refusing to match someone's chaos with your own

That's not weakness. That's **emotional leadership**.

Final Thoughts

You'll still react sometimes. We all do.

But the magic is in recognizing when it happens, pausing, and saying:

"Wait. Let me try again."

That moment of self-awareness—that breath, that shift—is the heart of real communication.

It's where your power lives.
It's where relationships begin to heal.
And it's how you become the calm in the middle of the storm.

Chapter Six

Speak with Clarity, Not Confusion

Say what you mean without watering it down
The power of short, honest, boundary-based phrases

Have you ever found yourself in a conversation where you felt like you were talking—but the other person just didn't get it? Maybe you said a lot, but nothing really landed. Or maybe you noticed you were trying to soften your message so much that it lost its meaning altogether.

That's the tricky trap of unclear communication. It's easy to fall into *confusion* when our words don't match our intent.

This chapter is about cutting through the noise. About **speaking clearly, honestly, and firmly**—without diluting your truth.

Why We Water Down What We Want

Most of us do this without even realizing it. We soften our words because:

- We don't want to hurt feelings

- We're afraid of conflict

- We worry about being "too much" or "too harsh"

- We want to be liked or accepted

But here's the irony: **watering down your message often creates more confusion, not less.**

People don't read minds.

They don't hear the *subtext* or the "nice way" you're trying to say something.

And when your true meaning gets lost, frustration grows—on both sides.

The Power of Clear, Concise Communication

When you speak with clarity, you make it easier for others to understand you and respect your boundaries.

That means:

- **Saying what you mean** without extra fluff

- **Using short, direct phrases** that hold weight

- **Owning your feelings and needs** without blame or apology

You don't have to be rude or harsh to be clear.

You just have to be *intentional*.

Examples of Clarity vs. Confusion

Confused:

"I guess it's fine if you want to stay out late again, but maybe if you don't mind, I'd prefer if you came home earlier sometimes."

Clear:

"I need you to come home by 10 PM tonight."

Confused:

"I'm not sure if this is a good time, but maybe we could talk about what happened later?"

Clear:

"I want to talk about what happened, but I need us to wait until we're both calm."

Confused:

"I just feel like sometimes you don't listen to me very well, but I guess maybe I'm being too sensitive."

Clear:

"When you interrupt me, I feel unheard. Please let me finish before you respond."

See the difference? Clear phrases leave no room for guessing. They tell the other person exactly what you mean, with respect and strength.

How to Craft Clear, Boundary-Based Phrases

Here's a simple formula to help you speak with clarity:

[State your feeling] + [State your need or boundary] + [Optional: State consequence or request]

Example:

- "I feel overwhelmed when plans change last minute. Please let me know at least a day ahead."

- "I need quiet time after work to recharge. I'll talk when I'm ready."

- "I feel disrespected when I'm interrupted. Please wait until I'm done speaking."

Why Short Phrases Work

Short phrases pack a punch because they:

- Are easier to process

- Avoid overwhelming the listener

- Help you stay calm and centered

- Prevent confusion and misinterpretation

Long explanations often invite debate or excuses. Short and clear communicates respect for both your needs and the listener's time.

Practice: Own Your Words with "I" Statements

Using "I" statements keeps your message focused on your experience rather than blaming the other person. It's one of the simplest ways to improve clarity.

Try replacing "You always..." or "You never..." with "I feel..." or "I need..."

For example:

- Instead of "You never listen," say "I feel unheard when I'm interrupted."

- Instead of "You're always late," say "I get anxious when plans start late."

When Clarity Meets Compassion

Being clear doesn't mean you have to be cold. You can hold your boundaries firmly *and* show care.

For example:

- "I'm upset that you forgot our plans, but I still want to work this out."

- "I need some space right now, but I care about resolving this."

Final Thought: Clarity Creates Connection

Clear communication isn't about winning arguments or proving points.

It's about **making yourself understood** so that true connection and respect can grow.

When you speak clearly, you invite others to listen more deeply. You give your relationship a chance to thrive—not just survive.

Chapter Seven

Boundaries Without Walls

How to say no with strength and compassion
Turning discomfort into confidence

Boundaries are the invisible lines that protect our well-being, define our values, and show others how to treat us. But often, when we think of boundaries, we imagine walls—cold, rigid, and unyielding barriers that push people away.

What if boundaries could feel different? What if they could be firm *and* warm? Strong *and* kind? This chapter is about building **boundaries without walls**—clear limits that create connection, not distance.

Why Boundaries Matter

Boundaries aren't just about keeping others out—they're about protecting *your* space to be authentic and respected. When you set healthy boundaries, you're saying:

- "I matter."

- "My feelings matter."

- "My time and energy are valuable."

Without boundaries, you risk feeling overwhelmed, resentful, or invisible. And ironically, lack of boundaries often leads to the very disconnection you're trying to avoid.

The Challenge: Saying No Without Guilt

Many of us struggle to say no because we worry about hurting others, disappointing people, or sparking conflict. Saying no can feel like rejection—something we fear.

But here's the truth:

Saying no is not selfish. It's a form of self-respect. And when done with compassion, it *builds* trust rather than breaks it.

Saying No With Strength and Compassion

How do you say no without feeling harsh or cold? How do you hold your line *and* keep your heart open?

Here are a few key practices:

1. Be Clear and Direct

Avoid vague or wishy-washy responses that invite confusion.
Example:

- Instead of "Maybe I can," say "No, I won't be able to."

2. Use "I" Statements

Frame your no around your needs or limits, not the other person's requests.

Example:

- "I'm feeling overwhelmed and need to rest tonight."

3. Express Appreciation

Acknowledge the other person's feelings or invitation before saying no.

Example:

- "Thanks for thinking of me, but I won't be able to join."

4. Offer Alternatives When Possible

If you want to maintain connection, suggest a different way to engage.

Example:

- "I can't meet today, but let's find time this weekend."

Turning Discomfort Into Confidence

It's normal to feel uncomfortable when setting boundaries—especially if you're not used to it. You might worry about being judged or disliked. But discomfort doesn't mean you're doing it wrong. It means you're growing.

Every time you say no kindly and firmly, you build a muscle of confidence. You teach yourself and others how to respect your limits.

Real Talk: Boundaries Don't Always Please Everyone

It's important to accept that **not everyone will like your boundaries**—and that's okay. Boundaries aren't about controlling others; they're about honoring yourself.

If someone reacts negatively, remember:

- Their feelings are theirs to manage, not yours to fix.

- You deserve respect, even if they disagree.

- Firm kindness is a powerful form of love.

Practice: Simple Boundary Phrases to Start With

Try these phrases to practice saying no with compassion and strength:

- "I appreciate you asking, but I can't commit right now."

- "That doesn't work for me, thank you for understanding."

- "I need to take care of myself, so I won't be able to."

- "I'm setting a boundary around my time and won't be available then."

When Boundaries Build Connection

Healthy boundaries actually improve relationships because they:

- Reduce resentment and misunderstandings

- Create clear expectations

- Build mutual respect and trust

When you set boundaries without walls, you invite others to meet you with honesty and care. You build bridges, not barriers.

Final Thought: Your Boundaries Are an Act of Love

Setting boundaries is one of the kindest things you can do—for yourself and for those around you. You're modeling self-respect and teaching others how to love you well.

Chapter Eight

Listen to Understand, Not to Win

Replacing rebuttals with reflection
Becoming the calmest person in the room

We often enter conversations—especially difficult ones—with the goal to *win*. To prove a point. To be heard and validated. But when arguing becomes a battle, everyone loses. Words fly, tempers flare, and real connection slips away.

What if the goal shifted? What if instead of trying to win, you aimed simply to *understand*? This chapter is about transforming how you listen—not as a weapon, but as a bridge.

Why We Don't Really Listen

The truth is, most of us don't *really* listen during conflict. Our brains are busy preparing what we want to say next, or rehearsing rebuttals to defend ourselves. When this happens, we miss what the other person is truly feeling and saying.

Listening to respond, rather than to understand, keeps us locked in a loop of defensiveness and misunderstanding.

What Does Listening to Understand Look Like?

Listening to understand means *being fully present*—putting aside your own agenda and genuinely hearing the other person's experience.

It's about:

- **Quieting your internal voice:** Pause your own thoughts and judgements.

- **Reflecting back:** Paraphrase or summarize what you hear to confirm understanding.

- **Validating feelings:** Acknowledge the emotions behind the words, even if you don't agree.

- **Asking curious questions:** Seek clarity, not confrontation.

Replacing Rebuttals With Reflection

When someone says something that triggers you, your first instinct might be to jump in with a counterpoint or correction. But this usually escalates tension.

Try this instead:

- **Pause.** Take a breath before responding.

- **Reflect.** Say, "What I'm hearing you say is..." or "It sounds like you're feeling..."

- **Confirm.** Ask, "Is that right?" or "Am I understanding you correctly?"

This simple switch from reacting to reflecting can defuse conflict and create a space where both people feel heard.

Becoming the Calmest Person in the Room

Listening deeply requires emotional control—staying calm when emotions run high. This isn't about suppressing your feelings, but managing your responses so you don't add fuel to the fire.

Here's how to become that calm presence:

- **Focus on your breath:** Slow, steady breathing grounds your nervous system.

- **Notice your body:** Recognize tension or agitation and consciously relax those muscles.

- **Anchor in empathy:** Remember that the other person's feelings are valid and real to them.

- **Stay curious:** Approach the conversation as a chance to learn, not to win.

By mastering your own calm, you invite others to lower their defenses too.

Why This Changes Everything

When you listen to understand:

- Arguments turn into conversations

- Defensive walls soften

- You build trust and respect

- Solutions become possible

It's a powerful skill that shifts the energy of any difficult discussion.

Practice: Active Listening Prompts

Try these phrases to practice listening with understanding:

- "Help me understand what you mean."

- "It sounds like you're upset because..."

- "I want to make sure I'm hearing you right."

- "Tell me more about how that made you feel."

Real Talk: Listening Doesn't Mean Agreeing

Important to remember: Listening to understand isn't the same as agreeing. You can hear someone fully without compromising your own truth.

The goal is connection—not surrender.

Final Thought: Listening Is Love in Action

When you listen without judgment or interruption, you say: "I see you. I hear you. You matter."

That simple act of love can transform even the hardest conversations.

Chapter Nine

Control Is an Illusion

Why trying to "fix" or "convince" never works
What real influence looks like in conversation

We all want to be heard, understood, and respected. In the heat of conflict or tough conversations, it's tempting to try to *control* the outcome — to fix the other person's view, change their mind, or steer the conversation exactly where we want it to go.

But here's the hard truth: **Control is an illusion.** No matter how persuasive you are, you cannot force someone else to see things your way. Trying to do so often backfires, making people dig in their heels, resist, or shut down.

Why Trying to "Fix" or "Convince" Doesn't Work

When you step into a conversation with the mindset of "I need to fix this" or "I have to convince you," you're operating from a place of power struggle. This can lead to:

- **Resistance:** People naturally push back when they feel manipulated or pressured.

- **Escalation:** Attempts to control can escalate conflict rather than resolve it.

- **Disconnect:** The focus shifts from connection to winning, leaving both parties feeling unheard.

Control fuels tension because it ignores the other person's autonomy—their right to think, feel, and respond in their own way.

What Real Influence Looks Like

Real influence doesn't come from force or persuasion. It comes from **connection, empathy, and authenticity.**

Influence is about:

- **Being present:** Showing up with genuine curiosity and respect.

- **Listening deeply:** Understanding where the other person is coming from, even if you disagree.

- **Expressing yourself clearly:** Sharing your truth honestly, without blame or attack.

- **Allowing space:** Giving room for the other person to process, respond, and choose.

When you let go of control, you create an environment where influence naturally happens. People are more open to hearing you when they don't feel pressured or cornered.

The Freedom of Letting Go

Letting go of the need to control can feel scary. It means trusting the process, and sometimes, accepting outcomes that aren't what you hoped for.

But here's the gift:

When you release control, you regain your **own** power—the power to choose your attitude, your words, and your response. That's true freedom.

Practical Tips for Letting Go of Control in Conversation

1. **Set intentions, not outcomes:** Focus on your intention to understand and be understood, rather

than forcing a specific result.

2. **Ask open questions:** Invite dialogue rather than debate. "What's your perspective on this?" instead of "Why don't you see it my way?"

3. **Accept emotions:** Recognize that feelings are valid, even if they're uncomfortable or inconvenient.

4. **Pause before reacting:** Give yourself a moment to breathe and reflect before responding.

5. **Focus on your circle of influence:** You can control your own words and actions, not others' reactions.

Real Talk: Influence Is a Process, Not a Power Move

Influence takes patience and humility. It's about planting seeds, not forcing growth overnight. Sometimes, just being steady and compassionate in the conversation is enough to open doors over time.

Final Thought: Control Is Overrated, Connection Isn't

In the dance of conversation, trying to control the steps leads to tension and missteps. But moving together with empathy and openness creates harmony and possibility.

Chapter Ten

Emotional Weight vs. Emotional Honesty

The difference between sharing and dumping
Communicating needs without overexposing yourself

In the heart of every meaningful conversation lies emotion. Sharing what we feel builds connection, trust, and understanding. But there's a fine line between *emotional honesty* and *emotional dumping*. Knowing the difference can save relationships from overwhelm and keeps communication healthy and respectful.

Emotional Honesty: The Gift of Clarity and Trust

Emotional honesty means sharing your feelings and needs in a way that invites understanding and connection. It's about being real without being reckless.

When you practice emotional honesty, you:

- **Own your feelings:** Speak from your experience using "I" statements rather than blaming.

- **Express needs clearly:** Let others know what you need in a way they can hear and respond to.

- **Maintain boundaries:** Share enough to be authentic, but not so much that it becomes overwhelming.

- **Build intimacy:** Create a space where vulnerability is safe and welcomed.

Emotional Weight: When Sharing Becomes Overload

Emotional weight is what happens when the sharing feels like a *dump* — heavy, unfiltered, and too much for the moment or listener to bear.

Signs you might be dumping:

- Sharing feelings in a way that feels overwhelming or relentless.

- Overloading conversations with negative emotions without pause.

- Using conversation as a way to offload all your stress without regard for the other person's capacity.

- Leaving the listener feeling helpless, drained, or responsible for fixing your feelings.

Dumping often leads to the other person feeling burdened, confused, or even shut down. It can create distance rather than closeness.

How to Share Honestly Without Overexposing

1. **Check in with yourself:** Before sharing, ask, "Am I expressing this to create connection, or am I just venting?"

2. **Choose timing wisely:** Some moments call for deep sharing; others call for lightness or space.

3. **Be mindful of your listener:** Consider their emotional bandwidth and readiness to engage.

4. **Use "I" statements:** Focus on your feelings and needs rather than assigning blame. For example, "I feel hurt when..." instead of "You always..."

5. **Keep it balanced:** Mix honesty with moments of gratitude, humor, or hope to keep the conversation from becoming too heavy.

6. **Invite dialogue:** Ask questions like, "Can I share something personal?" or "How are you feeling about what I'm saying?" to create mutual space.

Why This Matters

When you master the balance between emotional honesty and emotional weight, your relationships become stronger, more resilient, and more fulfilling.

You communicate what you need without overwhelming others. You build trust by being genuine but respectful of emotional boundaries.

Real Talk: Vulnerability Isn't About Overloading

Being vulnerable isn't about unloading everything all at once. It's about pacing yourself, honoring the other person's capacity, and creating a safe space for both to be seen and heard.

Practice: Emotional Honesty Framework

Try this simple guide when you want to share:

- **Name your feeling:** "I'm feeling [emotion]..."

- **Explain briefly why:** "...because [reason]."

- **State your need:** "What I need right now is..."

- **Invite connection:** "Does that make sense to you?" or "How do you feel about that?"

Final Thought: Honesty with Heart Creates Connection

When you communicate with emotional honesty, you build bridges instead of walls. You invite empathy and deepen your relationships—without the heavy baggage of emotional weight.

Chapter Eleven

Navigating Difficult People Calmly

How to protect your energy
Tools for keeping composure with manipulators or gaslighters

Some people drain your energy the moment they enter the room. Others leave you questioning your memory, your value, or your sanity. These are the people who push your buttons, poke at your peace, and seem to thrive on keeping you emotionally off-balance. Whether it's a chronic manipulator, a subtle gaslighter, or someone who just doesn't know how to relate respectfully—how you respond matters more than how they behave.

Let's be clear: you can't always avoid difficult people. But you can learn to protect your energy and show up with calm, grounded strength.

Calm Is Your Superpower

Staying calm isn't weakness. It's clarity. It's choosing not to feed someone else's fire. When you stay grounded, you protect your peace—and often, you shift the dynamic completely.

Difficult people tend to escalate when they sense emotional reactivity. But when you don't give them what they expect—when you *don't* bite the hook—they lose control of the script.

Types of Difficult People and Their Tactics

You may encounter:

- **The Gaslighter:** Twists facts to make you doubt yourself.

- **The Manipulator:** Uses guilt, flattery, or passive aggression to control outcomes.

- **The Bully:** Overpowers through intimidation or volume.

- **The Victim:** Always suffering, never accountable.

- **The Narcissist:** Makes everything about them, disregards your feelings.

Recognizing these patterns is step one. The next step is learning how to hold your center when you're in their presence.

Tools to Keep Your Cool

1. **Name the Game (Privately):** Know what tactic is being used so you can respond with intention, not confusion. Don't call them out—just call it out *to yourself*.

    Example: "Ah, this is gaslighting. I don't need to defend what I know is true."

2. **Use the Gray Rock Method:** Be emotionally uninteresting. Stay neutral. Don't feed the drama.

    Instead of: "Why would you say that?! That's not true!"

    Try: "You're entitled to your opinion."

3. **Keep Responses Short and Neutral:** Difficult people thrive on emotional engagement. Detach with simple phrases like:

    - "I hear you."

    - "Let's talk about this another time."

- "I'm not available for this conversation right now."

4. **Breathe Before You Respond:** When triggered, pause. Inhale deeply. Exhale slowly. Give yourself the gift of space before words come out.

5. **Set and Reinforce Boundaries:**

    Example: "I'm happy to talk when we can do so respectfully."

    Repeat calmly. No need to explain five times—once is enough.

6. **Don't Argue with Delusions:** If someone is committed to misunderstanding you, stop trying to convince them. Let your peace speak louder than your defense.

Protecting Your Energy

- **Create mental distance:** Remind yourself, "This isn't mine to carry."

- **Visualize a boundary:** Imagine a clear, calm wall between your emotions and their behavior.

- **Ground yourself physically:** Plant your feet. Relax your jaw. Soften your shoulders. These simple cues tell your body you're safe.

- **Exit when needed:** You don't have to stay in every conversation. It's okay to walk away—literally or emotionally.

Reminder: Calm Isn't Compliance

Staying calm does *not* mean tolerating mistreatment. It means you get to choose how you show up. You stay grounded not to please them, but to protect *you*.

Practice: Go-to Phrases for Calm Power

Try memorizing a few emotionally neutral phrases you can use when caught off-guard:

- "Let's revisit this when emotions are lower."
- "I'm not going to argue about this."
- "That's your perspective. I see it differently."
- "We're not going to get anywhere like this."
- "I'm done with this conversation for now."

Final Thought: Don't Let Chaos Inside You

You can't stop someone from being who they are. But you can stop their chaos from living in your mind.

Protecting your peace isn't selfish—it's essential. And when you stay calm in the presence of manipulation, you become the one with true power.

Chapter Twelve

Hard Conversations Without the Drama

A step-by-step method to approach sensitive topics
What to say when you're scared to bring it up

We've all been there—heart pounding, voice shaky, playing out worst-case scenarios in our head. You have something important to say. Something real. But the fear of how it might land keeps you silent, or worse, reactive. Hard conversations are called "hard" for a reason. But when approached with clarity and compassion, they don't have to end in drama.

They can become doorways—to understanding, healing, or necessary change.

This chapter is your guide to walking through that doorway with courage, not chaos.

Why Hard Conversations Spiral

Most people go into difficult conversations with one of two mindsets:

- **"I have to fix this right now."** (which leads to pressure and panic), or

- **"They'll probably get defensive, so why even try?"** (which leads to avoidance).

Both are driven by fear.

The truth? You don't need to fix everything, and you don't need to predict their reaction. You just need to **show up with honesty and self-respect**.

Step-by-Step: The Calm Conversation Method

Step 1: Get Clear on *Why* You're Speaking Up

Ask yourself:

- Is this about being right—or being real?

- What outcome would feel healthy, not perfect?

Clarity on your "why" brings courage to your "how."

Step 2: Choose the Right Moment

Tense moods, distractions, or late-night hours aren't ideal. Look for a neutral time when emotions are steady and attention is available.

Example: "Hey, can we talk sometime later today? There's something I'd like to share."

Step 3: Open Gently, Not Defensively

Start by creating emotional safety. This disarms defensiveness and invites connection.

Example:

- "This isn't easy for me to bring up, but it matters."

- "I'm not blaming, I just want us to understand each other better."

Step 4: Use "I" Language, Not "You" Accusations

Replace blame with ownership. Speak from your own experience.

Instead of:

- "You never listen."

    Try:

- "I feel dismissed when I'm interrupted. I want to feel heard."

Step 5: Be Specific and Simple

Don't overload the conversation with five months of buildup. Stick to the moment or pattern you're addressing.

Example:
"I felt hurt when you canceled dinner last-minute without checking in. I value plans and follow-through—it helps me feel respected."

Step 6: Pause for Their Response

Let them speak. Really listen. Even if it's uncomfortable.

You can say:

- "I want to understand where you're coming from too."

- "Take your time—I know this might be hard to hear."

Step 7: Stay Grounded If It Gets Heated

If emotions rise, ground yourself. Breathe. Don't chase control. You can calmly say:

- "Let's pause and come back to this when we're both calmer."

- "I don't want this to turn into a fight. I'm here to connect, not clash."

Step 8: End With Mutual Respect

You don't need a perfect resolution—just a respectful close.

- "Thanks for listening. I know that wasn't easy."

- "Even if we don't fully agree, I'm glad we talked."

What to Say When You're Scared to Bring It Up

Here are scripts for those "I don't even know how to start" moments:

- "This feels awkward, but I don't want to keep it inside."

- "I've been sitting on this for a while because I care about you."

- "I'm not trying to fight—I'm trying to be real with you."

- "This conversation is hard for me, but I think it's important for us."

Remember: bravery isn't the absence of fear—it's speaking up *with* the fear present.

Final Thought: Keep the Door Open, Not the Drama

Hard conversations aren't about being fearless or flawless. They're about being honest without losing your peace. When you speak up from a place of truth—not attack—you change the dynamic, even if the outcome isn't perfect.

You don't need to argue harder. You just need to say what's real, clearly and calmly.

That's how trust grows. That's how healing begins.

Chapter Thirteen

Repairing After Rupture

What to do when you've messed up
Apologizing effectively without losing self-respect

Every relationship—romantic, professional, or personal—experiences rupture. We say something in anger. We ignore a need. We break a boundary. And then comes the aftermath: silence, distance, awkwardness... or worse, damage that keeps festering.

What separates healthy relationships from harmful ones isn't **how perfect you are**—it's how you **repair** when things go wrong.

This chapter is about owning your part with strength, not shame, and restoring trust without losing your dignity.

Why Rupture Happens

Conflict is human. So are mistakes. When emotions run high, even the best of us can:

- Snap at someone we care about

- Avoid hard truths

- Shut down instead of speak up

- Say things we don't truly mean

What matters most isn't *that* you messed up—but *how* you respond afterward.

The Myth of the "Perfect Apology"

We often think an apology should be dramatic or groveling to be meaningful. But real repair isn't about theatrics—it's about **truth, timing, and tone**.

An effective apology:

- Acknowledges impact, not just intent

- Avoids excuses or self-pity

- Restores connection, not control

Step-by-Step: The Respectful Repair Method

Step 1: Own It Fully

Drop the defensiveness. People want to feel heard more than they want you to be perfect.

Instead of:

"I didn't mean it that way."

Try:

"What I said hurt you—and that matters. I see that now."

Step 2: Validate Their Experience

Even if you disagree with their reaction, validate their emotions.

"I understand why that upset you. I would've felt the same."

"You didn't deserve that tone. It's okay to be hurt."

Validation doesn't mean agreeing with every word—it means honoring their reality.

Step 3: Apologize Without Self-Erasure

Be sincere without shrinking. Own your behavior while still holding your worth.

Try phrases like:

> "I'm sorry for how I spoke. That's not who I want to be with you."
>
> "I lost my patience, and that caused pain. I regret that deeply."

Don't spiral into shame. Growth lives in responsibility, not self-loathing.

Step 4: Don't Over-Explain or Justify

When you lead with "I was just tired..." or "I only said that because...," it dilutes the apology.

Let the apology breathe on its own. You can clarify later—**repair first, explain second.**

Step 5: Ask, Don't Assume

Give them space to express how they feel. Repair is a *dialogue*, not a monologue.

You can say:

> "Is there anything else you need me to hear?"
> "How can I make this right moving forward?"

It shows humility and willingness to grow.

Step 6: Change the Behavior

An apology without action is just noise. Real change happens in how you show up afterward:

- If you yelled, practice pausing next time.

- If you dismissed them, practice reflective listening.

- If you broke a promise, set realistic commitments going forward.

It's not about being flawless—it's about being **intentional**.

What If They're Still Upset?

That's okay. You're not in control of their healing timeline—only your integrity.

Say:

> "I understand if you're not ready to talk yet. I just want you to know I care and I'm here."

Patience is part of repair. Let them process.

Self-Respect in the Repair Process

Apologizing doesn't make you weak. In fact, it's a sign of emotional maturity and strength.

But **losing yourself in guilt** is not the goal. The goal is reconnection—with them, and with your own values.

You can apologize *without*:

- Over-apologizing for your existence

- Taking blame for what's not yours

- Pleading for forgiveness

Speak the truth. Offer peace. Let go of control.

Final Thought: Rupture Isn't the End

If you're willing to take responsibility and repair with grace, ruptures can actually **deepen** a relationship. They can show the other person that even when things go wrong, you care enough to come back and try again.

Mistakes don't define you.

How you handle them does.

Chapter Fourteen

Leading with Calm in Any Room

Building your presence and credibility
Being the steady voice people trust

You've probably been in a room where someone walks in—and without raising their voice or taking up much space, they immediately shift the energy. People pause. They listen. There's something grounding about them.

That's not magic. That's presence. And it's built on calm.

In a world addicted to noise, defensiveness, and speed, *calm is power*. This chapter is about how to lead with it—at home, at work, in conflict, and in everyday conversation.

Why Calm Is Magnetic

People don't follow loud. They follow *steady*.

Calm leaders—whether they're managers, parents, friends, or partners—don't have to control the room. They regulate themselves first. And by doing that, they set the emotional tone for everyone else.

Your nervous system speaks louder than your words.

When you're calm, you:

- **Earn credibility without dominance**

- **Diffuse tension without saying much**

- **Hold boundaries without emotional backlash**

This doesn't mean being emotionless. It means being emotionally anchored.

What Leading with Calm Looks Like

It's not about being "zen" all the time. Leading with calm means:

- Listening without jumping to defend

- Speaking clearly, not forcefully

- Making space instead of scrambling for it

- Allowing tension without reacting to it

It's responding, not absorbing. Holding the room, not controlling it.

Practice 1: Ground Before You Enter

Before walking into a conversation, a meeting, or a conflict, **set your emotional tone on purpose**.

Ask yourself:

- What energy do I want to bring into this space?

- Who do I want to be, regardless of what happens?

- What is *mine* to carry—and what isn't?

Take three deep breaths. Drop your shoulders. Remind yourself: *I choose how I show up.*

Practice 2: Anchor to Your Values, Not Their Volume

People might get loud. They might get reactive. But their tone doesn't have to dictate yours.

Instead of matching intensity, **match your integrity**.

Try:

> "I hear how strongly you feel about this. I'm going to stay calm so we can move forward."

Your calm isn't a weakness. It's emotional leadership.

Practice 3: Speak Low, Speak Slow

Fast talk and raised voices escalate the nervous system. Calm lives in the opposite.

Lower your tone. Slow your rhythm. Choose shorter, intentional sentences like:

- "Let's take a minute."

- "I want to understand you."

- "Here's what matters to me right now."

When you slow down, people listen harder.

Practice 4: Make Space for Silence

You don't have to fill every pause.

In fact, people trust you more when you can sit with silence. It signals confidence, thoughtfulness, and emotional maturity.

If a conversation gets heated, try:

A pause. A breath. A nod.

Sometimes the most powerful message is your *non-reaction*.

Practice 5: Own Your Energy

Your energy leads before your logic does.

When you bring calm energy, others instinctively adjust. You signal safety. You signal, "We're okay. We can solve this."

Even if they don't consciously realize it, they'll mirror you over time.

That's the influence. And it starts with you.

Calm Is Not Passive—It's Intentional

Being calm isn't being soft. It's being in charge of yourself.

You can be calm and still:

- Set firm boundaries

- Disagree confidently

- Lead difficult conversations

- Inspire action

You're not minimizing conflict. You're creating the conditions to navigate it wisely.

Leading with Calm Changes the Room

When you regulate yourself, you *lead emotionally*. You become the person people want to talk to when everything's falling apart. The one they trust in moments of chaos. The one who brings clarity, not confusion.

And that? That's rare.

Be the calmest person in the room—and watch how others begin to rise to meet you there.

Chapter Fifteen

Your Voice, Fully Activated

Speaking up, setting limits, and showing up
Living aligned with your communication values

There's a moment in life—sometimes quiet, sometimes loud—when you realize: *It's time to stop editing myself to keep the peace.*

Your voice isn't just about the words you say. It's about who you become when you stop holding back.

This chapter is about activating that voice—not the reactive one that bursts out in anger or fear—but the steady, integrated voice that reflects who you are. The voice that speaks with clarity, sets boundaries with grace, and makes you proud when you walk away from a conversation.

Let's get to it.

What It Means to Be "Fully Activated"

A fully activated voice doesn't mean you talk more—it means you speak from alignment.

When your voice is activated:

- You don't shrink to make others comfortable.

- You don't explode to feel powerful.

- You speak from your values, not your wounds.

You stop second-guessing yourself in real-time. You say the hard thing, kindly. You express yourself without over-explaining. And you learn to sit with the discomfort of honesty—because it's worth it.

The Three Elements of Voice Activation

1. Self-permission

You can't speak what you don't believe you're allowed to say. Activation starts with internal permission: *I matter. My needs are real. My words are worth hearing.*

2. Emotional regulation

Activated doesn't mean agitated. Your voice has more power when it's calm, clear, and grounded.

3. Communication alignment

When your words match your values and your tone matches your intention, that's alignment. That's when your voice feels like *you*.

Speaking Up: No More Shrinking

If you've ever walked away from a conversation thinking *"I should've said something…"*—you're not alone.

Many of us are taught that being "nice" means being quiet. But there's nothing kind about betraying yourself for someone else's comfort.

To speak up, ask yourself:

- What truth am I holding back?

- What would I say if I trusted myself more?

- What am I afraid will happen if I'm fully honest?

Now speak to the situation, not from your fear. Practice phrases like:

- "Here's what I need to say, even if it's hard."

- "I want to be real with you about something."

- "This matters to me, and I want to share it clearly."

Setting Limits: Boundaries That Sound Like You

A fully activated voice includes the power to say *no*—not with apology, but with ownership.

Instead of:

- "I'm sorry, I just can't..."

  Try:

- "That doesn't work for me."

- "I need to hold this boundary, even if it's uncomfortable."

Boundaries don't require justification. They just require truth. When your voice is aligned, you stop over-explaining your limits. You speak them simply and stand by them with grace.

Showing Up: Using Your Voice When It Counts

Sometimes the hardest thing isn't saying what you feel—it's being consistent with it.

Living in alignment with your communication values means:

- You speak the truth, even when your voice shakes.

- You don't weaponize silence or play mind games.

- You follow through on what you say, or you own it when you don't.

Your integrity becomes part of your tone.

You're not here to perform. You're here to *connect*—honestly, respectfully, and courageously.

Activating Your Voice in Everyday Moments

- **In meetings:** Speak before you're "ready." The right words come when you trust your presence, not your perfection.

- **With loved ones:** Don't wait for a blowup. Use your voice daily to set expectations, express gratitude, or raise concerns early.

- **With yourself:** Notice the inner critic. Replace it with self-talk that encourages strength and clarity.

Try this:

"My voice doesn't need to be perfect to be powerful."

"I can say the hard thing and still be kind."

"I deserve to be heard, even if not everyone agrees."

Your Voice Is a Gift—Use It

When you activate your voice, you activate your life.

You stop pretending, performing, or pleasing your way through relationships. You start trusting that the people who belong in your life will meet you in your truth.

And the more you speak from your center, the less you fear rejection. Why? Because you're no longer betraying *yourself*.

Final Thought

Your voice isn't a weapon—it's a bridge.

And when it's fully activated, it becomes one of your most honest, beautiful forms of leadership.

Let people hear you—not the version you think they want, but the version that's true. The version that honors your values. The version that sets you free.

Made in United States
Orlando, FL
19 July 2025